Meet the Computer

J.G. Seal

Head of Mathematics
Summerbee Secondary School
Bournemouth

Stanley Thornes (Publishers) Ltd

© text J.G. Seal 1982

© diagrams ST(P) Ltd 1982

All rights reserved. No part of this publication may be reproduced, stored in a retrieval system, or transmitted in any form or by any means, electronic, mechanical, photocopying, recording or otherwise, without the prior written consent of the copyright holders.

First published 1982 by
Stanley Thornes (Publishers) Ltd,
Educa House,
Old Station Drive,
Leckhampton Road,
Cheltenham, GL53 0DN.

British Library Cataloguing in Publication Data

Seal, J.G.
   Meet the computer.
   Pupil's workbook
   1. Electronic digital computers
   I. Title
   001.64   QA76.5

ISBN 0-85950-384-4

ACKNOWLEDGEMENTS

The authors and publishers are grateful to the following who provided photographs and gave permission for reproduction:

Barclays Bank Picture Library (page 7); Barnaby's Picture Library (pages 1 and 14); British Airways (page 22); Central Electricity Generating Board (page 2—bottom); The Department of Computer Science, University of Manchester (page 2—top); Ford Motor Company Ltd (page 19); Rank Strand Ltd (page 26); The Wiggins Teape Group Ltd (page 23).

We also wish to thank the Cheltenham & Gloucester Building Society for providing us with the outline artwork for the map on page 8.

Typeset by Factel Ltd, Cheltenham.
Printed and bound in Great Britain by Ebenezer Baylis & Son Ltd, Worcester.

Contents

CHAPTER		PAGE
1	An Excellent Memory	1
2	A Fast Worker	6
3	A Super Sausage Machine	10
4	Do As I Say	15
5	The Search for Knowledge	18
6	Real Time and Let's Pretend	21
7	Fun and Games	26

An Excellent Memory

You will probably have seen many pocket calculators similar to the one in the picture. Perhaps you own one yourself.

A typical pocket calculator

If you enter a number into a calculator it will remember it. The number will stay in the calculator, and will appear on the display, until something happens to change the situation. If you use the number in a calculation, or clear the calculator, or switch it off — or if the batteries run down — the number will usually be lost. On some calculators, however, it will be stored even if the calculator *is* switched off. On others, especially the more expensive ones, there are extra memories so that numbers can be remembered even while a calculation is going on. But even the most elaborate calculators can store only a few numbers — usually no more than three, though occasionally up to eight or ten.

A computer, on the other hand, even a small one, can store thousands of numbers, and other information as well — lists of names, for example, or the instructions a robot requires to spray a car with paint, and even instructions for the computer itself to follow. This ability to store

A very early computer built at Manchester University

A modern mainframe computer

large amounts of information, or **DATA**, is one of the ways in which a computer is different from a calculator.

In the early days, computers were all very large. To store even quite small amounts of data required a great deal of space. Over the years, however, it has become possible to make computers smaller and smaller as new technology has been developed. There are still many very big computers in use where especially large amounts of data have to be dealt with, or very complex calculations have to be performed, or where several people have to get at the data at the same time. But the needs of ordinary computer users can now be met by much smaller machines, some of them so small as to be portable.

The largest computers, often occupying several fixed cabinets standing in a special computer room, are often called **MAINFRAME COMPUTERS**. The smallest ones are usually known as **MICROCOMPUTERS**.

When a computer is switched off it will usually forget the data in it, just as most calculators will. The internal memory, or **MAIN STORE**, generally works only as long as the power is on. So a computer has access to other memory, called **BACKING STORE**, which keeps its contents even when the power is switched off. Data from the main store is copied into the backing store if it is to be kept, or if the main store is full. Backing store can be of several kinds. Most microcomputers use tape cassettes, or magnetic **FLOPPY DISCS**, as backing store.

Because computers can hold a great deal of information they are used in all sorts of organisations. Here are some examples.

(Some spaces have been left for you to add to the list more examples of the kinds of information which could be stored on a computer at your school.)

Where they are Used	Examples of the Kind of Information they Store
Factories	Details of all the nuts and bolts and other items held in stock. The wages to be paid to each worker each week, together with the tax and insurance deductions to be made from each.
Police headquarters	The names of known criminals, and details of the crimes for which they have been convicted.
Banks and Building Societies	Details of the accounts of each customer.
Schools	Form lists. Examination results. . . . .

Because computers are so widely used now, people often have their names and information about them of one sort or another in the memories of several computers. If they have bank accounts, the details will be in computers. Their employers may keep information about them in computers. If they have driving licences, they will be on computer files at the Licensing Centre. If they have any hire purchase agreements, the details will be in the computers run by the hire purchase companies.

The data in each of these computers will be protected by access codes, or passwords. Only someone knowing the codes will be able to get at it. But even so, a lot of people are worried that so much information about them is stored in computers. It might be possible for someone using a computer illegally to find out very personal things about someone else, perhaps in order to cheat that person of large sums of money. But remember that if the information were stored, not in a computer, but in an ordinary filing cabinet in an office, it would still be possible for someone with criminal ideas to get at it.

A computer has an excellent memory. But there is more to it than just the memory, and it can carry out all kinds of operations on the data held in it. As mentioned earlier, a computer can itself store the instructions which will make it carry out a particular operation. A set of instructions for a computer is called a **PROGRAM**. Different programs are used to make the computer do different things.

One very useful thing a computer can do is to sort a list of names into alphabetical order. Before we could write a program to make a computer do this we would have to be very clear that we knew how to do it ourselves.

Even if we were going to use a program written by someone else we would need to know the sort of result to expect so that we could check that the computer was doing the job properly.

Here is a list of the names of a small French class, and the marks they got in a test.

J. Thompson	47
M. Rose	36
C. Adams	81
T. Dudley	18
G. Adlam	46
L. Francis	29
P. Rose	92
J. Bedford	47
N. Jameson	49
D. Richardson	61

Write out the list of names in alphabetical order.

....
....
....
....
....
....
....
....
....
....

While we are at it, let us do some other things with this data that we could, if we wished, get a computer to do for us.

Write out the list of names in mark order, with the person who had the highest mark first.

....
....
....
....
....
....
....
....
....
....

Find the total marks of all the members of the class.

Total = ...

What is the mean (average) mark of the class?

Mean = ...

Use the information in the mark list to complete the block graph.

All these activities—sorting, calculating, drawing graphs—can be undertaken by a computer.

No. of pupils

0–19 20–39 40–59 60–79 80–100
Marks

END OF CHAPTER EXERCISE

In this chapter a number of important words have been printed in upper case (capital) letters. These words are listed below, and are followed by a set of sentences. There is a sentence to match each word or word pair, but they are not in the right order. Carefully copy each sentence into the space beside the matching words.

DATA ....

....

MAINFRAME COMPUTER ....

....

MICROCOMPUTER ....

....

MAIN STORE ....

....

BACKING STORE ....

....

FLOPPY DISC ....

....

PROGRAM ....

....

(a) The memory in which a computer first stores the data put into it, and which usually forgets its contents when the computer is switched off.
(b) An example of backing store.
(c) A list of instructions for the computer to follow.
(d) A large computer used by an organisation which has need of a great deal of computing power.
(e) A memory to which data is transferred if it is to be kept when the computer is switched off, or if the main store is full.
(f) Numbers, words, or other information.
(g) A very small computer, sometimes portable.

A Fast Worker

We have seen that a computer can store large amounts of data. We have also seen some of the things that can be done with stored information—sorting into alphabetical or numerical order, calculating averages, drawing block graphs. In this chapter we shall look at two further examples of data processing in which the speed, and accuracy, of the computer are of great importance.

In our first example, let us imagine that we are organising a hockey competition for five teams. Each team has to play each of the other teams once.

How many matches must each team play?

Number of matches = ...

How many matches will there be altogether?

Total number of matches = ...

We are going to plan the competition so that no team ever plays in two consecutive matches. It will thus be possible to play two matches in one afternoon.

One possible way of arranging the matches is as follows. We shall call the teams A, B, C, D and E for simplicity.

> A v E
> B v C
> D v E
> A v B
> C v D
> B v E
> A v C
> B v D
> C v E
> A v D

You will find that if there are only four teams it is not possible to arrange the competition so that no team ever plays in two consecutive matches. Try it, and see if you can work out why it is not possible.

Then try to plan a competition for six teams A, B, C, D, E and F, again with the rules that each team plays every other team once, and that no team plays in two consecutive matches.

Number of matches for each team = ...

Total number of matches   = ...

Fixture list:

... v ...

... v ...

... v ...

... v ...

... v ...

... v ...

... v ...

... v ...

... v ...

... v ...

... v ...

... v ...

... v ...

... v ...

... v ...

... v ...

... v ...

... v ...

... v ...

... v ...

Space has been left for 20 matches, but you will not need them all.

With five or more teams it is always possible to plan a competition in this way. But if you had to work out a plan for, say, ten teams, it would take you a very long time, and it would be encouraging to know that it could be done before you started.

How many matches would you have to plan for ten teams?

Total number of matches = ...

A computer would be a great help here. A program could be written to make the computer sort teams into pairs according to any rules you choose — provided it was not expected to do the impossible. And once the program was written, it would be able to work out a plan for any possible number of teams very quickly indeed.

Let us look now at our second example, the use of a computer in a bank. Here speed, in working out the accounts of thousands of customers, is again very important, and accuracy, too, is a vital necessity.

The bank will use the computer not only to keep a list of its customers and how much they each have in the bank, but also to record the amounts

A computer terminal in use in a bank

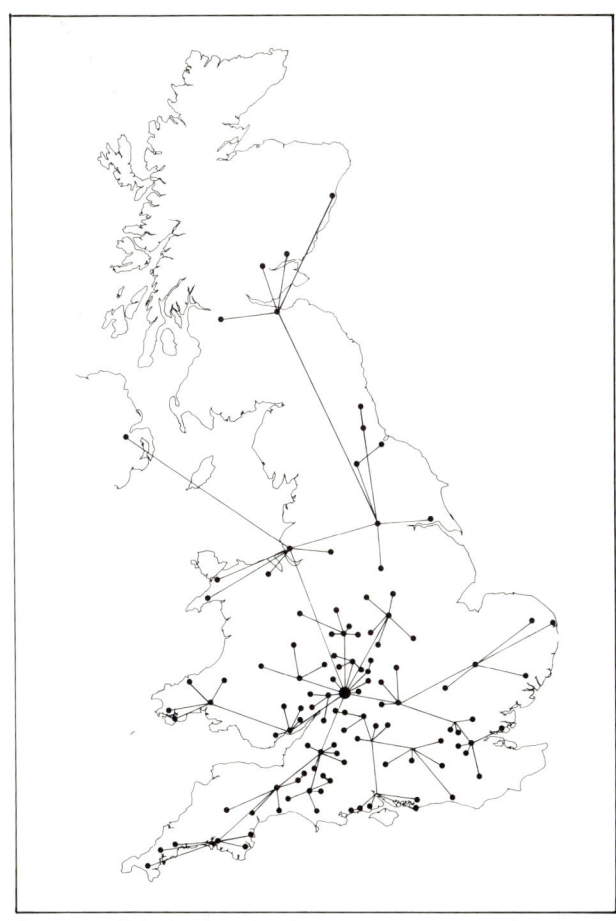

A map of Britain showing the computer network operated by a building society with headquarters in Cheltenham

paid into and withdrawn from each customer's account. Illustrated below is part of a bank statement, showing the details of a customer's account.

The statement has several columns. The numbers, like 197483, in the 'Particulars' column, are the numbers of cheques which the customer has written to make payments from the account. Whenever entries are made in the account the balance is brought up to date at the end of the day by adding money received or subtracting money paid out. 'ABBEY NAT B/S' is an abbreviation for Abbey National Building Society, and this payment is a regular monthly one in respect of a mortgage. The customer borrowed money from the building society to buy a house and is repaying it in this way. 'S/O' means 'Standing Order', which is a way of making regular payments from a bank account without having to write a cheque each time. 'SUNDRY CREDIT' refers to money paid into the account over the counter in the bank. 'YORK-GEN UNIT TST' indicates that money has been paid as a premium on a life assurance policy with the Yorkshire General Assurance Company.

Date	Particulars		Payments	Receipts	Balance *When overdrawn marked OD*
1980	Opening Balance				874:37
15OCT		197483	55:97		
		197485	1:91		816:49
17OCT		435289	197:07		619:42
20OCT	ABBEY NAT B/S	S/O	97:47		521:95
21OCT		197487	51:91		
	BNMTH TELEPHONES	S/O	24:00		446:04
22OCT		197486	2:99		
		435269	38:25		
		435291	72:06		332:74
23OCT		197484	20:00		
		197490	4:14		308:60
24OCT		197488	25:35		283:25
27OCT	SUNDRY CREDIT			286:37	
		197489	11:90		
		435294	50:00		507:72
28OCT		197491	1:89		
		197493	25:48		
	YORK-GEN UNIT TST	S/O	8:25		472:10
29OCT		435293	3:45		468:65

Work out the daily balances for the bank statement extract below.

Date	Particulars		Payments		Receipts		Balance *When overdrawn marked OD*	
1981	Opening Balance						3509	60
16 DEC		669064	50	00				
		669077	2014	00				
17 DEC		669078	12	00				
		669079	30	00				
18 DEC		560348	29	00				
		669062	2	00				
21 DEC	SUNDRY CREDIT				344	52		
		669086	100	00				
	ABBEY NAT B/S	S/O	97	47				
	BNMTH TELEPHONES	S/O	21	50				
22 DEC		669065	5	96				
		669066	5	05				
		669080	50	00				

ASSIGNMENT

Find something about computers in a paper or magazine — an advertisement, a picture with a caption, or an article. If you can find more than one, so much the better. Put your cuttings in an envelope, or mount them on a sheet of thin card or sugar paper so that they can be displayed. The most interesting item would be an article, with pictures, on recent developments in the computer world, but these are not very easy to find.

A Super Sausage Machine

A computer is a machine which can remember a great deal of information and perform all sorts of operations on that information. But it is just a machine. It has to be programmed—told exactly what to do—and cannot have any bright ideas of its own.

In a way it is like a sausage machine. Put meat in at one end of a sausage machine, together with whatever else is needed to make sausages, and out at the other end come sausages. Put a list of names in random order into a computer and, if it has the right program, out at the other end comes a list of those names in alphabetical order.

A big difference between a sausage machine and a computer, of course, is that the sausage machine can only turn out sausages, while a computer can be made to turn out something quite different just by changing the program. Instead of a complete list of names in alphabetical order it could produce the names beginning with W, or count the number of times the letter E occurs in the list. Another important difference is that a computer can remember so much more than a sausage machine!

We can draw a simple block diagram to show the main parts of a computer system.

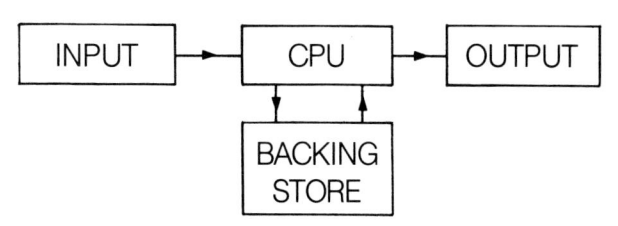

INPUT	→	CPU	→	OUTPUT
		↕		
		BACKING STORE		

The box in the middle marked CPU is the heart of the whole system. CPU stands for **CENTRAL PROCESSING UNIT**. The CPU can be thought of as having three parts:

ARITHMETIC UNIT
CONTROL UNIT
MAIN STORE

In the arithmetic unit, or logic unit as it is sometimes called, the working out and sorting take place. Here, for example, numbers can be added together, or words can be put into alphabetical order.

The control unit ensures that the computer carries out in the correct order the instructions in the program.

The main store, or immediate access store, is the memory where the program and all the data immediately needed are stored.

INPUT to most microcomputers is by means of a keyboard, like a typewriter keyboard; **OUTPUT** is on a screen; and backing store is a cassette tape or floppy disc. However, a keyboard is not the only way information can be communicated to a computer, and a screen is not the only form of output used. There are also other forms of backing store.

Input Devices

Instead of using a keyboard to input data directly to a computer, we can arrange for the data to be typed first on to **PUNCHED CARDS** or **PAPER TAPE**, and for a **CARD READER** or **PAPER TAPE READER** to transfer the data from the cards or tape to the CPU. Each column on a card, or each row across a paper tape represents a code for a particular figure, letter, or other character. A card reader can read cards with incredible speed—up to 2000 cards a minute. Each card holds 80 characters, so you can work out how many characters per minute can be input to a computer in this way.

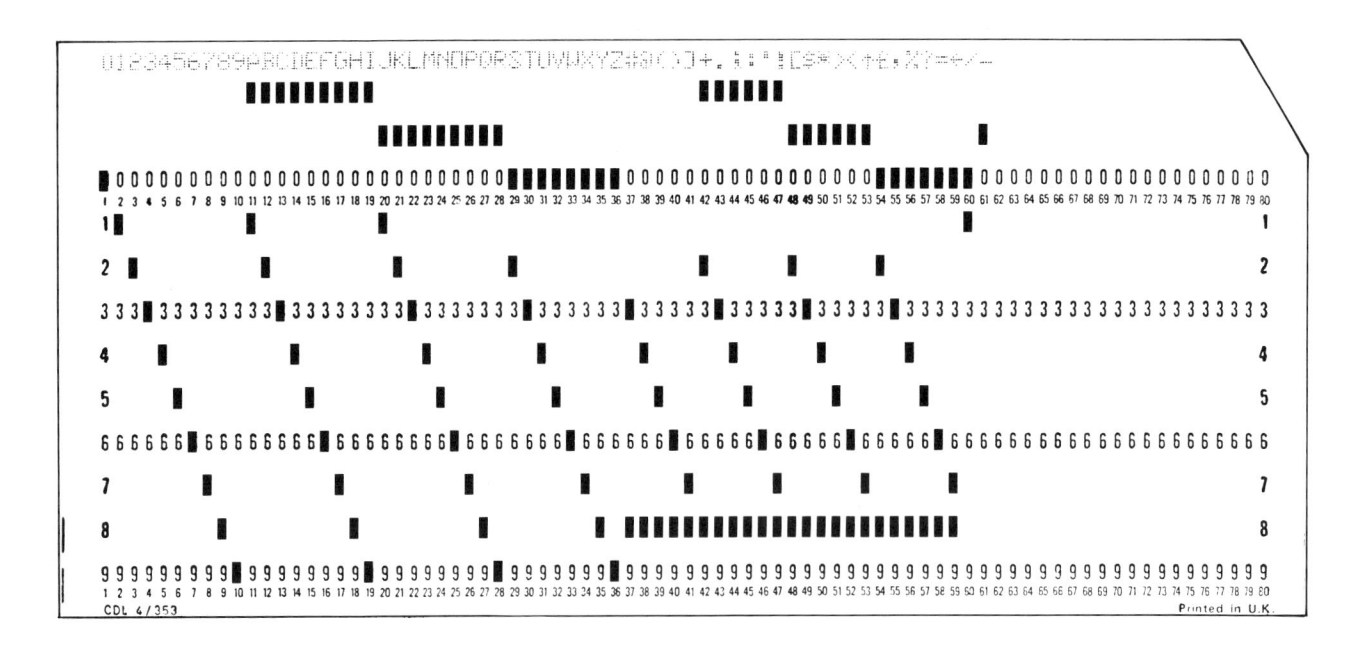

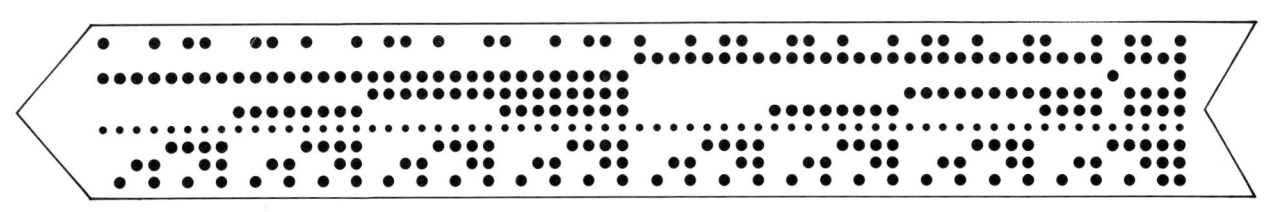

A Punched Card, showing the hole patterns for each of the characters, and a sample of Punched Paper Tape.

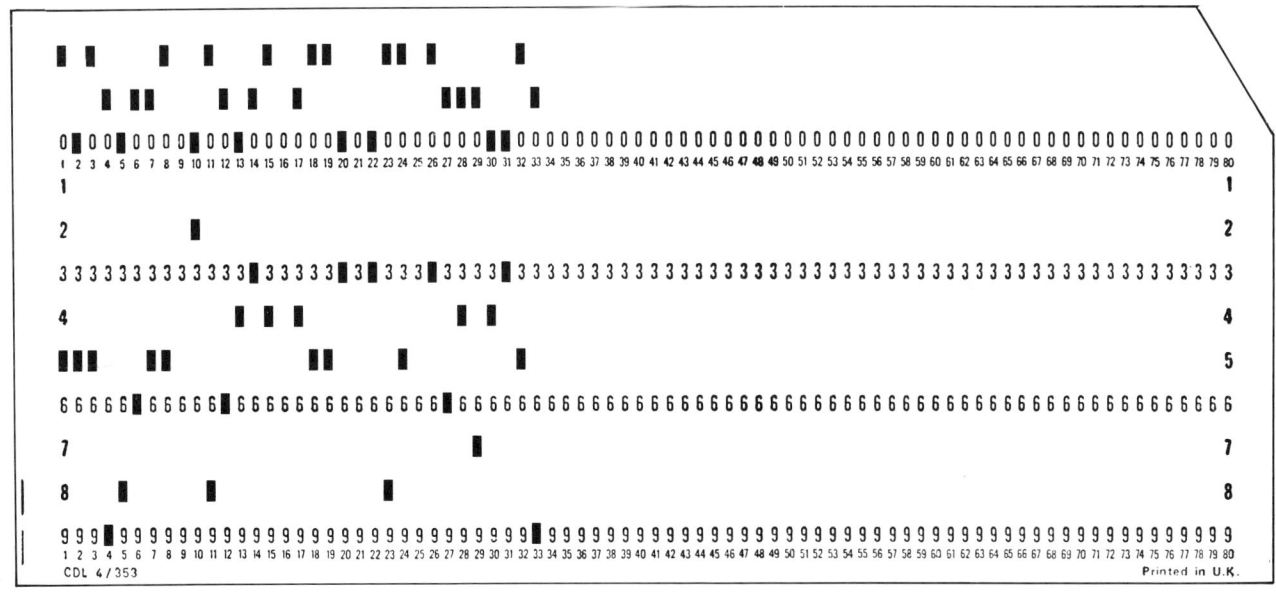

Paper tape readers are not so fast, but even they can input up to 90 000 characters a minute.

Typists working the card and tape punch machines are much slower than the card and tape readers, so several typists could put data on to cards or paper tape to feed one computer.

The card illustrated above has had a message punched into it. Use the card on the previous page as a key to decode the message.

The message: ....

....

Sometimes magnetic tapes are used instead of paper tapes to input data, and there are other devices, such as light pens, which we shall be looking at later in the course.

Output Devices

A screen, or **VISUAL DISPLAY UNIT** (VDU), is a very convenient way of looking at the output of a computer, but it does not give a permanent record. When this is needed, a printer is connected to the computer. There are many different types of printer. Some are like typewriters. They include the golf-ball and daisy-

A line printer

wheel printers. These printers are quite slow in operation and with the ability to print only a limited range of characters. Others, such as the **LINE PRINTER**, are very much quicker. The line printer depends for its speed on the fact that a whole line of output is printed in one operation, unlike a typewriter, which prints one letter at a time. A good line printer can print up to 1500 lines a minute, with 120 characters on each line. A common type of printer for use with microcomputers is the **DOT MATRIX PRINTER**, which creates a wide range of characters and can even produce pictures, by printing patterns of small dots very close together. These vary in speed from about 30 to 100 characters per second.

Complete this table, which shows the speeds in characters per second and characters per minute of various input and output devices.

Device	Characters per second	Characters per minute
Paper tape reader		
Card reader		
Daisy-wheel printer	60	
Dot matrix printer		6000
Line printer		

It would be interesting to compare the speed at which you write with the speed of operation of these readers and printers.

Copy out the sentence below for exactly 30 seconds. Stop when the time is up, even if you have not finished the sentence. Count the number of letters and spaces you have written. Write neatly at your normal speed.

A computer is a machine which can remember

. . . .

a great deal of information and perform

. . . .

all sorts of operations on that information.

. . . .

Number of characters in 30 seconds = ...

Number of characters per minute   = ...

Other output devices include graph plotters, which can actually draw lines and can be used to make graphs and engineering drawings, and card and tape punches.

Backing Store

We have already mentioned two forms of backing store used by microcomputers — cassette tape and floppy disc. Larger computers often use reel-to-reel magnetic tape (which is like music tape, but wider), and disc stacks. The amount of data which can be held on one of these devices is difficult to visualise. An ordinary five-disc stack can hold 200 million characters. A telephone directory holds about 10 million characters. You can work out how many telephone directories could be stored on one disc stack:

    Number of directories = ...

Input and output devices and backing stores are all called **PERIPHERALS** — they surround, and are controlled by, the CPU, but are not actually part of it.

RAM, ROM and BYTES

The main store, or immediate access store, is usually made up of two different kinds of

A disc stack being loaded into a disc drive

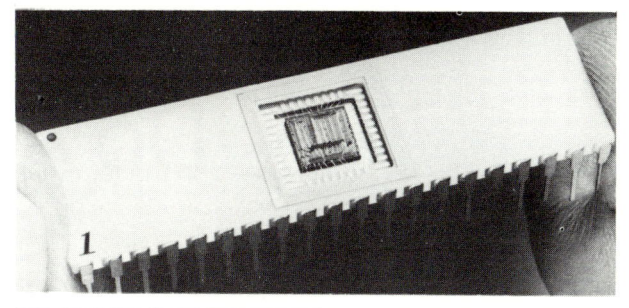

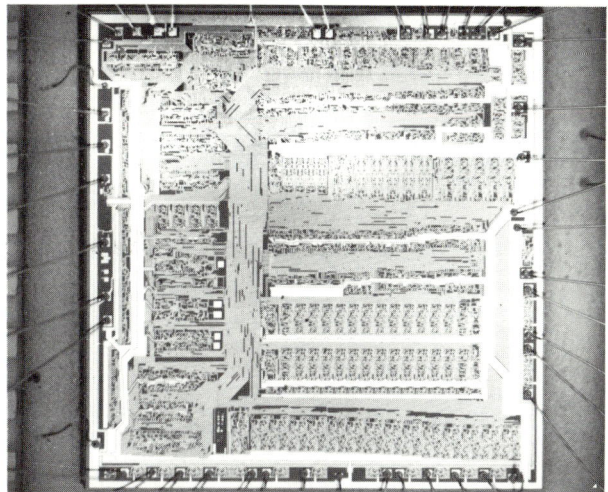

An integrated circuit — the whole package above, and a microphotograph of the silicon chip itself below

memory, **RAM** and **ROM**. RAM stands for 'Random Access Memory'. Information stored in this memory can be changed merely by overwriting what is already in it with new information, and information anywhere in the memory can be accessed (got at) at any time. This is different from holding information on a tape. To get at that you would have to wind through the tape till you found the piece you wanted. The information held in RAM is lost when the computer is switched off, as explained in Chapter 1.

ROM stands for 'Read Only Memory'. This information cannot be changed by overwriting it with new data, and it is not lost when the computer is switched off. ROM contains the instructions which the computer always needs — what to do when the word RUN is typed in, for example. The ROM is contained in a 'chip' in the computer and is supplied with it by the manufacturer.

Each piece of memory large enough to hold one character is called a **BYTE**. A computer with 8k bytes (8 'kilobytes') of memory can hold about 8000 characters.

14

Do As I Say

When we want a computer to carry out a particular operation we have to give it precise instructions. The instructions form a program, and are written in a **PROGRAMMING LANGUAGE**.

There are many different programming languages, each designed to meet particular needs. Here are a few of them:

FORTRAN From the words FORmula TRANslation; used in scientific research and mathematics.

ALGOL An ALGOrithmic Language; also used in science and mathematics.

COBOL A COmmon Business Oriented Language.

CESIL The Computer Education in Schools Introductory Language.

PASCAL A language designed to aid precise, structured programming (named after Blaise Pascal, an early experimenter with mechanical calculating machines).

We shall have a look at a language called **BASIC**—which stands for Beginner's All-purpose Symbolic Instruction Code, though don't let that put you off!

BASIC instructions are very much like instructions in English and are thus easy to memorise and to put together in a program. For example, the instruction

20 PRINT "MY NAME IS JOHN"

will tell the computer to do just that. Notice the number at the beginning of the line. Each line in a BASIC program starts with a line number like this, and the computer normally carries out the instructions in line number order. Notice also the quotation marks round the string of characters which the computer has to print.

The line above, on its own, is not really very useful, but print statements like it are useful as part of a bigger program. Consider this one:

10 PRINT "ENTER YOUR AGE IN YEARS"
20 INPUT A
30 LET M = A * 12
40 PRINT M
50 END

This program could be entered into a computer at the keyboard. If the command RUN is then typed in, the computer will execute (carry out) the instructions in the program. This is what it does:

It first executes line 10 and puts the words ENTER YOUR AGE IN YEARS up on the screen. We call this 'printing' even when no printer is connected to the computer.

Next, the computer executes line 20, which tells it to wait for a number to be input at the keyboard. When the number is entered it is stored in the main store at a memory location labelled A.

At line 30, the number in A is multiplied by 12, and the answer is stored at location M.

At line 40, the number in M is printed out. BASIC programs usually end with an END or STOP statement (line 50).

Notice the use of * for multiply. Can you think of a good reason for using * instead of ×?

It will be seen that this program will print out the number of months you have lived up to your last birthday. The program would be improved if it said this when it printed out the result. We could alter line 40 to the following:

40 PRINT "NUMBER OF MONTHS TO LAST BIRTHDAY = "; M

To change line 40 to this new version in the computer we would merely type it in again. This would delete the old version as the new one was entered.

The new line 40 instructs the computer to print out the string of characters   NUMBER OF MONTHS TO LAST BIRTHDAY =   followed by the number stored in M.

The programs written for a computer are collectively called **SOFTWARE**. The computer itself, and its peripherals, are called **HARDWARE**.

END OF CHAPTER EXERCISE

A The following program contains a number of errors. If you have studied this chapter carefully you should be able to write it out again correctly.

10 PRINT "ENTER A NUMBER
20 A INPUT
30 LET S = AXA
40 PRINT THE SQUARE OF YOUR
   NUMBER IS S

. . . .

. . . .

. . . .

. . . .

16

B If the numbers 6 and 11 are input to this program, in that order, what numbers will be printed out?

    1Ø PRINT "ENTER TWO NUMBERS"
    2Ø INPUT A
    3Ø INPUT B
    4Ø LET D = A * A
    5Ø LET E = B * B
    6Ø LET F = D + E
    7Ø LET G = E – D
    8Ø PRINT F, G
    9Ø END

    Numbers printed out: . . . .

Do this again, using the numbers 5 and 3 as input, in that order.

    Numbers printed out: . . . .

C Write a program which will instruct the computer to ask users to enter the year they were born and will then calculate and print out how many years old they are on their birthday this year.

. . . .

. . . .

. . . .

. . . .

. . . .

D Write a program which will instruct the computer to ask users to input two numbers and will then multiply the numbers together and print out the answer.

. . . .

. . . .

. . . .

. . . .

. . . .

. . . .

E Write a program of your own choice to input numbers, calculate with them in some way, and print out the result. Here are some suggestions:
    (a) Input cost of one book and number of books bought, output total cost.
    (b) Input number of pens bought and total cost, output cost of one pen.
    (c) Input length and width of rectangle, output perimeter and area.
    (d) Input five numbers and output their mean (average).

The Search for Knowledge

Humans are for ever striving to learn more and more about the world we live in and the universe of which the world is a part. The search for knowledge has taken people to the moon, and we have sent space vehicles to distant planets to be our eyes where we cannot go ourselves.

We have explored the macrocosm, the vastness of the heavens, but we have also looked into the microcosm, the smallness of living cells, and at the molecules which cells are made of. And by the clever use of sophisticated apparatus much has been discovered about things which are too small to see at all—about atoms, the building blocks of matter, and about even smaller particles of which the atoms themselves are made.

The knowledge gained in these explorations has been put to use to build machines which help the process of exploration itself. Knowledge of light and how light travels led to the development of the telescope and the microscope. Knowledge of electrons led to the development of the radio telescope and the electron microscope.

The spade, the plough, the steam hammer and the motor car helped people physically by adding to the power of human muscles. The telescope and the microscope added to the power of human eyes. The telephone and radio added to the power to communicate with other people at a distance. And now we have the computer, adding to the power of the human brain.

Scientists today have in the computer a tool which the scientists of only forty years ago did not have, a tool with a vast memory and incredible powers to sort out and calculate. Scientists working on the development of a new way to produce power, for example, or a new drug to combat disease, or a new shape for a high-speed train, can use computers to store the information they need and to carry out with great rapidity all the complex calculations they have to do. But the computer can do other things as well.

Using a **LIGHT PEN** a designer can draw a shape on a VDU screen, or alter a shape already in the computer's memory. The computer can be programmed to show the shape from different angles, or to calculate the wind resistance to the shape at different speeds.

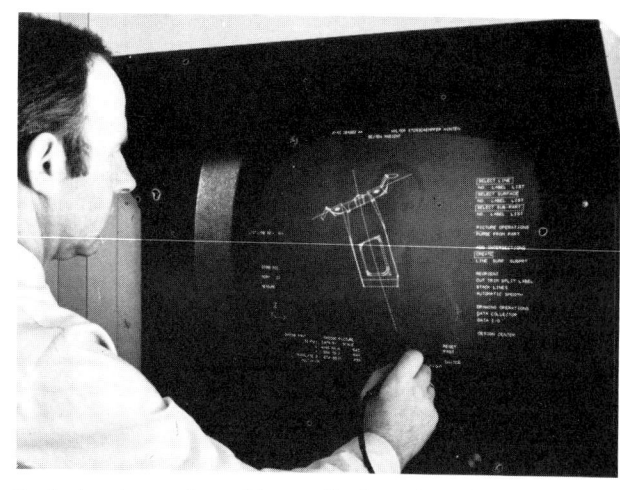

Part of a piece of machinery displayed on the VDU. The designer can easily change the size of the drawing and the angle it is viewed from, and can alter the shape itself, by writing on the screen with the light pen

Using a **GRAPH PLOTTER** the computer could then draw on paper the shape which had been displayed on the VDU.

The search for knowledge goes on not only among scientists in research centres, but also among pupils at school, and students at college, and computers can help here too. Computer programs have been written to enable pupils to practise their multiplication tables, or to help them to learn their French vocabulary, and for many other purposes. **COMPUTER-ASSISTED LEARNING** (CAL) is being tried out in many situations. This computer course is itself an example.

There is also **COMPUTER-MANAGED LEARNING** (CML) in which a computer is used to help a teacher to keep records of pupils' work and to plan a course which is best suited to the needs of each individual pupil.

A designer using a light pen

END OF CHAPTER EXERCISE

At the end of Chapter 1 you copied out sentences to explain the important words in that chapter.

Here is a list of some of the important words from Chapters 2 to 5. Next to each one write a sentence of your own to explain what it means.

CPU ....

....

ARITHMETIC UNIT ....

....

CONTROL UNIT ....

....

CARD READER ....

....

LINE PRINTER ....

....

VDU ....

....

PERIPHERAL ....

....

LIGHT PEN ....

....

GRAPH PLOTTER ....

....

CAL ....

....

6.
Real Time and Let's Pretend

A computer can be used in several ways.

It can be used for **BATCH PROCESSING**. In this mode, a number of programs are entered into the computer and run, one after the other. To save computer time the programs are usually typed first on to punched cards or paper tape, and then entered through a card or tape reader.

Batch processing is often used when a school has access to a computer at a nearby college. Pupils write out their programs on either special coding sheets or pieces of lined or squared paper. A batch of these programs is sent to the computer centre, where they are typed on to punched cards. After the computer has run the programs the results are printed on a line printer and sent back to the school.

This diagram, which is a very simple form of flow chart, illustrates the batch processing system.

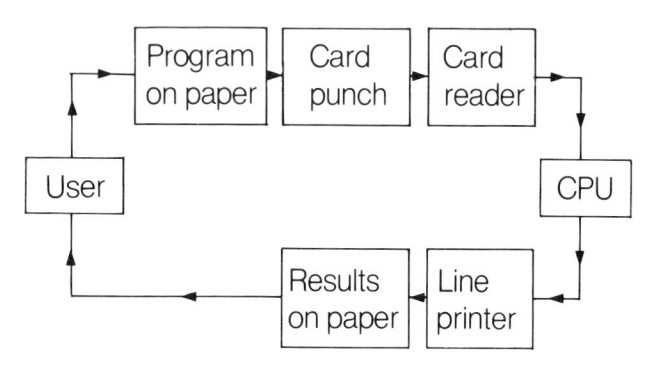

```
User → Program on paper → Card punch → Card reader → CPU → Line printer → Results on paper → User
```

Another way to use a computer is **ON-LINE**. That is to say, the computer is connected by wires, perhaps through a telephone line, to a **TERMINAL** (a keyboard with a VDU and/or a printer). The user enters the program at the terminal (or uses a program already stored in the computer) and gets the results on the VDU or printer as soon as the computer has run the program. A microcomputer is really in on-line mode all the time unless special arrangements are made to operate it in some other way.

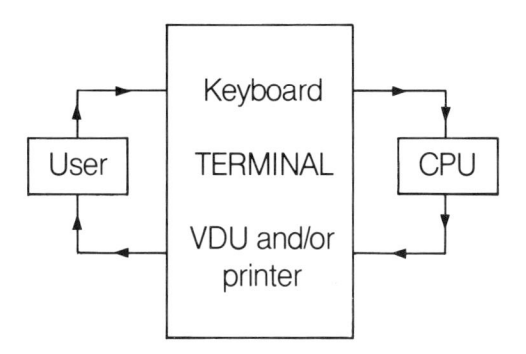

```
         ┌─────────────┐
         │  Keyboard   │
   User ─┤  TERMINAL   ├─ CPU
         │ VDU and/or  │
         │   printer   │
         └─────────────┘
```

Programs are often written so that messages are produced for users which tell them what to do next, or where a mistake has been made. Such a program is known as an **INTERACTIVE** program. Most work done on-line is interactive. A program which produces pleasant and easily understood messages is called 'friendly'.

When a program is run on a computer the results obtained depend on the data supplied. In the program given in Chapter 4 the data is the age of the user in years, and the result is the number of months lived, up to the last birthday. This data does not change very often — once a year, in fact — and it would not matter if the program were run just after the user's birthday, or eleven months later.

Sometimes, however, a computer depends on data which is continually changing, and then it has to run continuously in order to keep its memory up to date and produce accurate results. British Airways has a very large computer system called BABS which is used, among other things, to book passenger seats on its aircraft. BABS is on-line to terminals all over the world. If someone in New York wants to book a seat to London on a particular day, the booking clerk uses the terminal to find out if there are any spare seats on that day, and to make the booking if there are.

BABS has continuously to enter in its memory bookings made or cancelled so that it can always produce information which is up to date and accurate. This is called **REAL TIME** use of a computer.

An airline booking being made by computer

Another example of real time use of a computer is when one is used to control a process such as the moulding of plastics parts, or the making of a motor car. The computer is continuously fed data on what is happening in the process, and makes decisions as to what has to be done next.

Another very useful application of a computer is to make it **SIMULATE**, or imitate, a real life situation in order to find out what is likely to happen under various conditions. For example, it could simulate the way a new design of aircraft would fly at different speeds. It could pretend that an aircraft built to the new plans was flying at a particular speed and work out the stresses which the wings of the aircraft were undergoing. It could repeat the calculation for faster and faster speeds until the point was reached at which the wing would break up. This would be a much better way of finding the breaking point than sending up a pilot in a real aircraft!

The Central Electricity Generating Board uses a computer simulation to see what would happen to the electricity distribution system, the National Grid, if certain generators, switches, or power lines, were put out of action by lightning or some other cause.

A computer controlling the manufacture of photographic printing paper

The weather forecasting service uses a computer simulation to determine what weather is likely to occur.

The computer is sometimes blamed for putting people out of work. Because of its ability to remember and recall vast amounts of information, to control manufacturing processes, to work out in advance the probable results of experiments, or to help designers in their work, it has indeed reduced in some areas the number of people required. Against this, it must be remembered that the use of computers is usually cheaper than the use of people to achieve the same result, and that the development, manufacture, running, and maintenance of the computers themselves provide work for many people. It should also be remembered that computers have relieved many people from boring and repetitive jobs.

A Dice Simulation Experiment

Simple programs can be entered into a computer to simulate the throwing of a single dice, or of two dice together.

The graphs below and on the next page show the results obtained in runs of dice simulation programs. Notice the difference between the shapes of the two graphs.

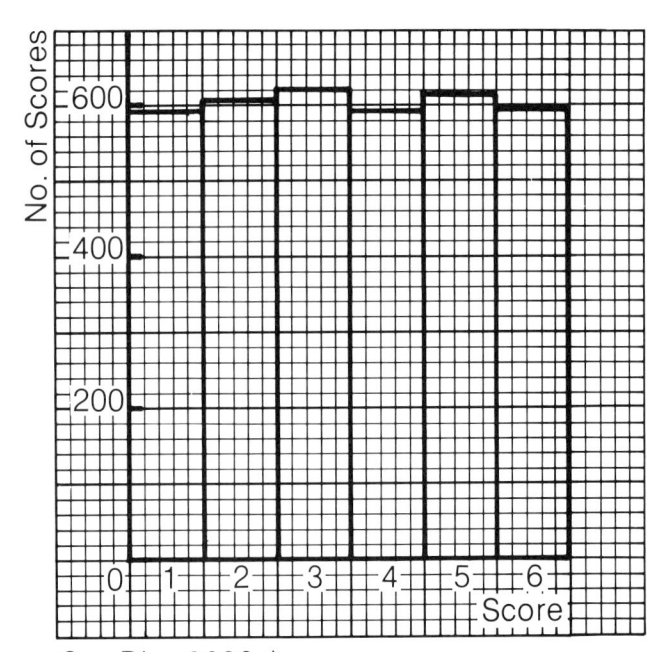

One Dice 3600 throws

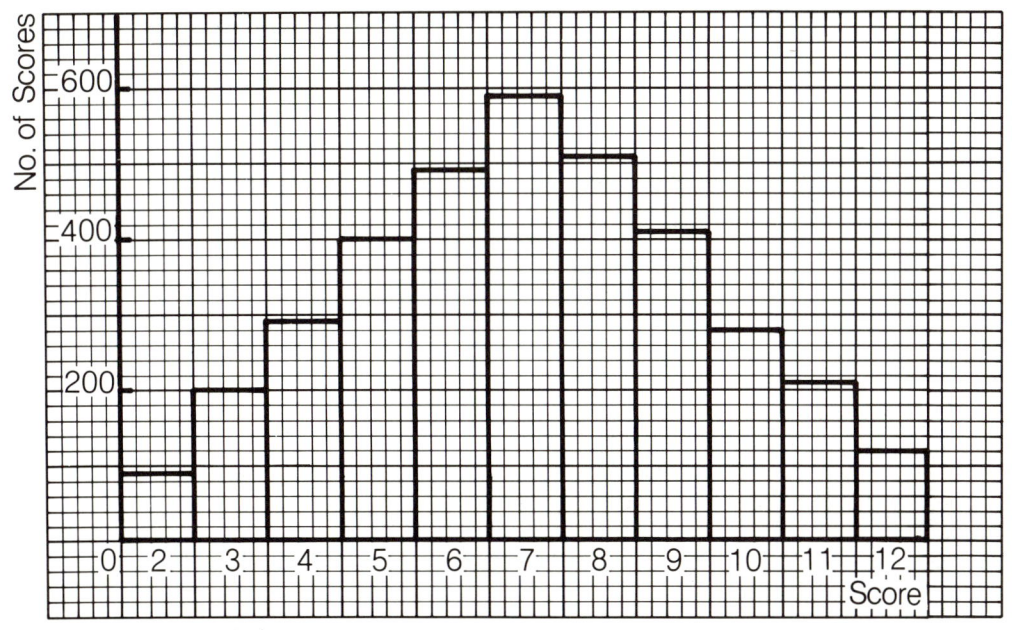

Two Dice 3600 throws

The following exercise may help you to understand the difference in shape.

This table shows the scores obtained when two dice, A and B, fall in different ways.

Dice B

	1	2	3	4	5	6
1			4			
2						
3				7		
4						
5						
6	7				11	

Dice A

When dice A comes up 1 and dice B comes up 3, the score is 4. When A comes up 3 and B comes up 4 the score is 7. Complete the table.

How many ways can a score of 6 be obtained?

Number of ways = ...

Now look at the next table. It shows the number of ways in which scores from 2 to 12 can be obtained.

Score	2	3	4	5	6	7	8	9	10	11	12
No. of ways					5						

Complete the table.

24

Use a computer to simulate 3600 throws of a single dice and of two dice. Enter the results below, and use them to complete the block graphs.

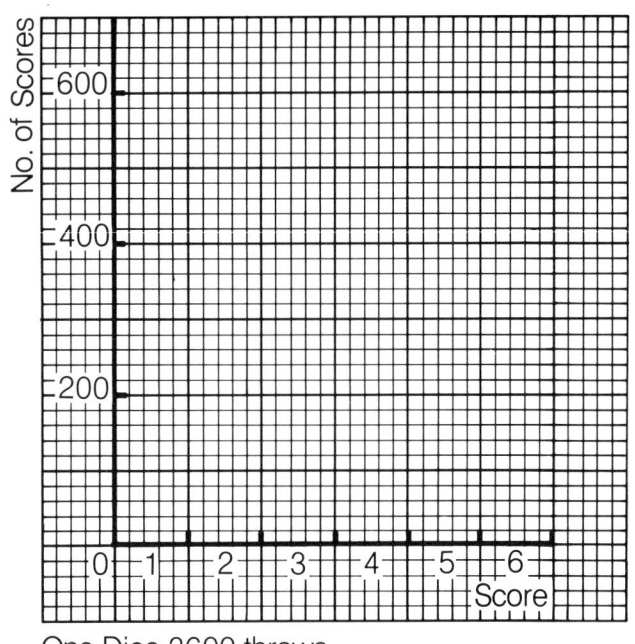

One Dice: total number of throws 3600

Score	1	2	3	4	5	6
No. of scores						

Two Dice: total number of throws 3600

Score	2	3	4	5	6	7	8	9	10	11	12
No. of scores											

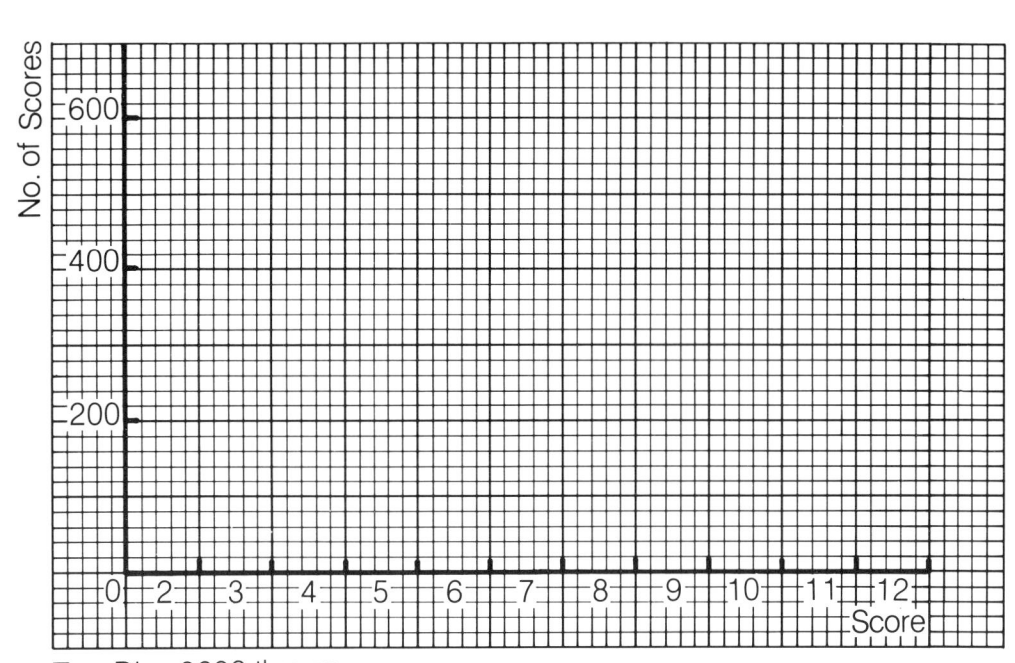

One Dice 3600 throws

Two Dice 3600 throws

25

Fun and Games

You will probably have played the computer game 'Space Invaders', or something similar. Games programs can be written for any computer, and computer magazines often print listings of games programs. Most games make use of **GRAPHICS**—pictures on the VDU screen. Games with animated graphics are especially popular, but it is possible to devise quite interesting games which do not involve graphics at all.

Many games are examples of simulations. The computer produces imaginary situations involving space ships, jungle animals, or ski slopes.

Computers can be used for leisure and pleasure in other ways as well. One possibility is to use a computer linked to a synthesiser to produce a succession of 'musical' sounds. Some computers in fact contain a loudspeaker and can produce the sounds on their own.

Computers can be used to control a display of coloured lights, and they are often used in the theatre to control the stage lighting.

A computer being used in the control of stage lighting

A number of experiments have been conducted in producing patterns or pictures using a computer. Some examples of such 'computer art' are given here.

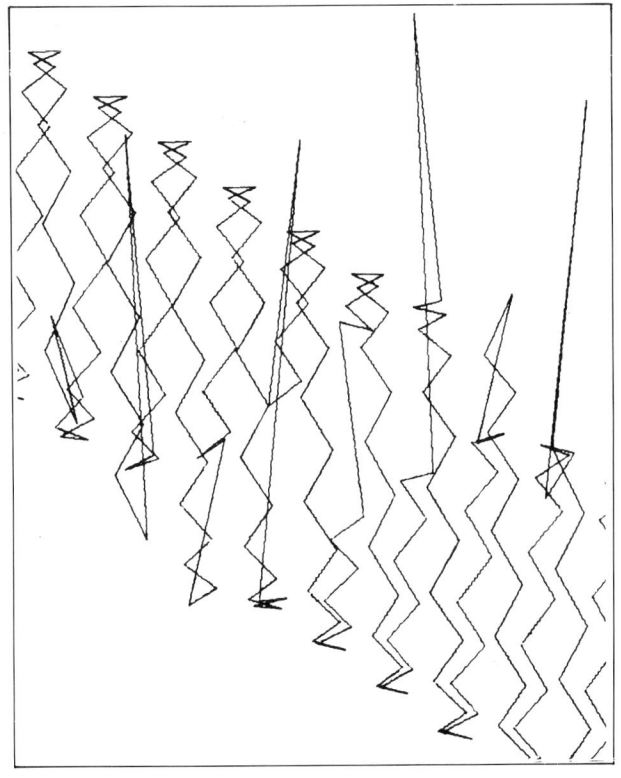

Dad's Army. This picture was drawn by a graph plotter controlled by a computer programmed to draw lines more or less at random. It was chosen from a batch of fifty pictures, most of which did not seem to mean anything at all

Cave Woman, Disco Dancer, or Tennis Star? This picture was produced on a dot-matrix printer by using different characters to give different degrees of shading. If you look at it from a distance of a metre or more you will find it easier to interpret

The computer is increasingly finding its way into ordinary homes where it can be used both seriously — for keeping family accounts, for study, and so on — or for pleasure — for games, art, music and for the fun of programming. A new development we are likely to hear much of in the next few years is the use of computers in conjunction with the television Ceefax and Oracle information systems. Computer programs for almost any purpose will be available for loading straight into a home computer through a television receiver.

In all this — the development of uses for computers — we are finding new things to interest us and occupy our leisure time, besides new ways of doing things which up to now have been time-consuming and perhaps boring. Playing games against a computer has already become very popular — almost habit-forming sometimes. There is perhaps a danger here that we may begin to consider computers as worthier or more interesting opponents than our friends, and may even begin to consider them as conscious brains. But as we have seen, computers cannot think their own thoughts. They merely carry out very quickly and accurately instructions given them in the form of a program, and that program is written in the first place by a human being. Even the development of programs which themselves produce other programs cannot remove the ultimate human responsibility for what computers do.

Computers are here, and they are not going to go away. On the contrary, they are going to become more and more a part of our lives. If we are to avoid being intimidated by them, we need to have some understanding of them.

In this short course we have covered a lot of ground. But we have not dealt with *how* computers work. We have not considered the electronics or the logic of computer circuits. We have not learned anything about the binary representation of numbers and other data, though computers store all information in binary form. If you want to learn about these matters you will be able to find other books which deal with them, and you may be able to take a longer course of computer studies, perhaps leading to a public examination.

Some of you may have discovered already how interesting programming can be, and will want to pursue the subject after this course is finished. Some of you may even have had the thought that you would like a career in computing, and this is certainly worth keeping in mind for the future.

To conclude, here is a quotation from the writer Morris West. It comes from his book *Harlequin* (Fontana, 1972), which is a novel based on the idea that a man who controls a large computer can, if he is dishonest, use his power for his own criminal ends, playing on the ignorance of others.

> 'The computer is a mighty brain, which can store centuries of knowledge, perform miracles of mathematics in the twinkling of an eye and deliver infallible answers to the most abstruse equations. In fact, it seduces man into blind faith and then betrays him to his own idiocy.'

FINAL EXERCISE

A Here are descriptions of two games which a computer could be quite easily programmed to play. Try playing them with a friend. One of you pretends to be the computer, and the other one is the user.

Game 1 GUESS
The 'computer' chooses any number from 1 to 800 inclusive, and writes it down, to avoid the possibility of later argument, but does not tell the user what the number is. The user tries to guess the number. All the 'computer' can say after each guess is whether it is correct, or too high, or too low. If you can discover the right method it will always be possible to find out what the number is in ten guesses or less.

A computer program for this game would instruct the computer to choose a number from 1 to 800 at random and store it in its memory. It would then invite guesses and reply to each guess much as the human 'computer' would, by printing out CORRECT, TOO HIGH, or TOO LOW. After ten wrong guesses it would tell you that you had lost, and invite you to have another try.

Game 2 WORD CHAIN
The user says any word. The 'computer' then says a word whose first letter is the same as the last letter of the first word. The user then thinks of a third word to continue the chain, and so on. For example, the first five words might be

COW   WATCH   HOUSE   EAGLE   EGG

Words may not be repeated in the same game. The player who fails to think of a word to continue the chain loses the game.

A computer program for this game would put, say, three words beginning with each letter of the alphabet into memory. When the computer has run out of words beginning, say, with F, you could win by giving it a word ending with F. Or the computer might beat you by producing a batch of words ending with X or Z!

B Here is a wordsearch containing fifteen words connected with computing. You have come across all of them during this course. Five of them are listed here. The other ten you will have to discover for yourself. See if you can ring all fifteen words.

The five you can start with are

    DATA   BYTE   PROGRAM   FORTRAN
    TERMINAL

```
A G D B I O C L H E G A F C J B K
B U T E R M I N A L F I E L A J H
J E J C I S A B L R O C E T J H D
G L M A I N F R A M E Z C U L C J
G E Q B A I B Q G C X H I E I E M
D E D G C D Y A W O G B P V A V D
Q H C B D A T A I F R F C I Q D H
E W E C B G E C P N A P K T R W G
H Y G F O R T R A N P L B C V E L
H S J C I A F B A F H U Z A J U P
S I M U L A T I O N I V T R K B J
E A R E T N I R P C C U E E J C G
U D J I L D H F A N S B M T U O G
J V I A P M H U H A P N Q N T E U
C B J F E P B F U E D I H I X Z D
```

C A computer crossword

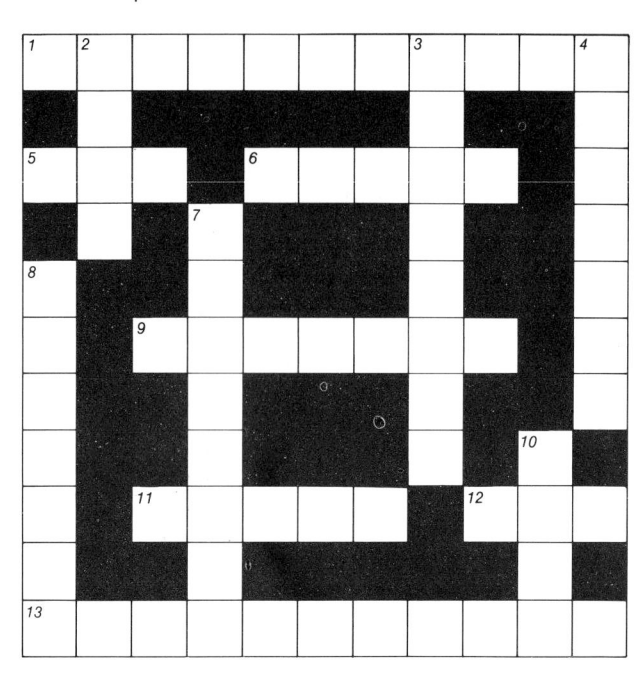

Here are the clues to the crossword:

Across
1. Capable of back-chat. (11)
5. A sort of cup at the heart of things. (3)
6. Short for a small one. (5)
9. Support a store for forget-me-nots. (7)
11. A pen easy to pick up? (5)
12. Run into, and read and write wherever you choose. (3)
13. Does words and numbers too, of course. (4,7)

Down
2. Could be the New All-Purpose Language. (4)
3. The end of the line for a computer. (8)
4. Carry out instructions to chop someone's head off. (7)
7. You won't get this from a toy watch. (4,4)
8. This unit ensures order. (7)
10. Re-order peat — it's full of holes. (4)